Having an
Affair with
Faith

DEON D. HAYES

One Vision Publishing

One Vision Publishing

Paperback ISBN: 978-0-578-18491-3

Library of Congress Control Number: 2016917380

PRINTED IN THE UNITED STATES OF AMERICA

Table of Contents

Acknowledgments i

Introduction... iii

Having an Affair with Faith..vii

1. The Pleasure of Pain and the Cost of My Anointing....1

2. Crazy Gets the Blessing 7

3. The Release 11

4. Basketball: The Teacher of Life 14

5. He Did It on Purpose..20

6. I Need a Lawyer 24

7. Favor with the Judge 34

8. I Need an Alternate Ending..39

9. I Ordained the Struggle..44

10. Keep Your Hands Clean and Behave Yourself
    Wisely 53

11. The Battle Was for You, but the Victory Was
    for the People 56

12. I've Got Enough Faith to Change the Verdict..........60

Acknowledgments

I want to thank GOD for writing a great story for my life, I appreciate every day every moment, every victory that I have is because of you. To my parents Willie and Janis Hayes, words are not enough to tell you how much I love you, how much I appreciate you and how greatful I am for everything that you have done for me, and the investments that you have made in me, I am who I am today because of you. To my wife Katrice I couldn't have created a better wife, you are the best, thank you for always being there for me, for always pushing me, for always believing in me, and for always celebrating my accomplishments, I love you forever. To my children Christian and Jennifer I love you both more than action or words can express, you motivate me to do better to be better, I'm so thankful to have the both of you as my children, I work hard for you appreciate life and live in the moment. To my Brother and my sisters Andrew, Tanya, Tamara, and Tyrine, I love you all so much, thanks for putting your life on hold to support my dreams and my vision, I pray that GOD grant you every desire of your heart. To my Church One Vision, every ounce of me loves you, I work hard for my church, you guys have prayed for me, labored with me, we've laughed together and we've cried together, I love you so much, thank you for supporting me and my family, thank you for trusting me as I follow the plan of GOD, we just getting started, greater is coming!

Introduction

Faith: Belief that does not rest on material evidence or logical proof.

I've often said, "Faith is not what you see, but faith is what you don't see."

You don't need faith to believe that the sky is blue; you can walk outside and see that it is blue. Faith is needed when GOD whispers a secret to you and you don't know how, you don't know when, and sometimes you don't know why, but because you've come to the realization of how powerful GOD is, you know that it will happen.

There are many occasions that have shaped my belief, but there is one that ignited it.

It was the late '80s, I was a teenager, my parents were going out, and I asked if I could stay home. I decided to cook something. Not having a lot of experience in the kitchen, I did not notice that there was grease on the stove. I turned the range on and before I knew it, the top of the stove was on fire.

My heart started racing, fear came over me, and I

panicked. It felt like my body was paralyzed. I couldn't think—all of the teaching I received in school concerning how to respond if there was a fire was nowhere to be found.

All of a sudden, I could hear the voice of my grandmother as if she was standing right next to me. My grandmother, a powerful woman of GOD, told me,

"Grandson, if you ever get in trouble and you don't know what to do, call on the name of JESUS."

Words are powerful; you can remember them even if you don't remember who said them. I opened my mouth and I said, "JESUS," and when I said it, one flame went down. I couldn't believe what was happening in front of my eyes. I looked around as if someone was there to witness what just happened. I said, "JESUS," again and another flame went down. I began to think if the name of JESUS has enough power to make two flames go down, I better keep saying it until all the flames have went down.

And so I kept saying the name of JESUS until every flame went down and before I knew it the fire was gone. What I didn't know was, while GOD was decreasing the flames on the stove, he was creating a flame in me, a flame of faith.

This was the experience that ignited not only my faith but my "crazy" faith.

The word crazy doesn't just mean to be affected with madness; it also means to deviate from moderation, to go from normal to abnormal, to be possessed by enthusiasm, to see what others can't see, to remove logical from your vocabulary. When GOD does great things, it doesn't always make sense, but you have to trust him even when people think you're crazy.

To get something crazy you've got to do something crazy, like the men who had been out all night fishing and JESUS told them to go back out and let down their net and prepare for a draught. *Draught* means catch, and *drought* means dry season. It amazes me how GOD can exchange one word and change your outcome.

The men had been out all night and didn't catch anything, but they said, "Nevertheless, at your word we will go back out." They went back out and there was so much fish, the Bible said their nets broke, and their boats began to sink.

I have a word for you today. GOD doesn't just want to break your net; he wants to break your net worth. Logic will paralyze you, but your ability to believe GOD for what doesn't make sense will be the thing that ultimately brings you to the place of overflow. To get something crazy, you gotta do something crazy. Always remember "crazy" gets the blessing.

Having an Affair with Faith

There was a little boy who would always climb a tree in the back of his house. He anticipated family gatherings so that he could demonstrate what he had practiced daily.

When he was successful in his endeavor his father would stand there proudly applauding with the rest of his family members, but when he would fall his father would abruptly escort the family members into the house.

When the boy became a man he decided to confront his father because he had been holding on to anger and resentment for some years now. He said to his father, "I've been angry for a long time now," and his father asked him, "What are you angry about?" The son responded, "When I climbed the tree and I was successful at it, you celebrated me, but when I fell and hurt myself, you led the family into the house because you were embarrassed."

His father responded, "Oh no, son, you don't understand. I wasn't embarrassed. I was trying to teach you two important lessons. The first lesson is pain is good, because it lets you know that you're still here; it's an indication that you haven't lost your ability to feel. For the second lesson, I asked the family to go in the house because I wanted to help you understand that you don't need an audience in order to get back up."

The first chapter of Exodus tells us that a new king arose over Egypt, one who did not know Joseph. The reason for the scripture pointing that out is because GOD prophetically speaks through the scriptures to let us know sometimes yesterday's victories will not suffice for today's battle. What went on in Joseph's time could not help the people at that time. GOD had to do a new thing.

The text tells us that the new king became intimidated by the children of Israel because they were fruitful, and increased abundantly, and multiplied, and waxed exceeding mighty;

And because of this he set over them taskmasters to afflict them with their burdens. My favorite part says, "But the more they afflicted them, the more they multiplied and grew."

In everything that you go through, in everything that the enemy attempts to destroy you with, make sure that your affliction does not stop you from multiplying and growing. Make sure you don't lose your enthusiasm about the promise GOD has given you just because you're being afflicted. Pain is an indication that the baby is coming.

We know that the 17th chapter of 1st Kings says that GOD sent ravens to bring Elijah food, but the majority of readers never ask why GOD sent ravens out of all the animals he could have chosen.

First, the scripture says that GOD "commanded" the raven. The word *command* is defined as: to give an order, to tell someone to do something, which means in order for GOD to command the ravens, he understands the language of animals and he can speak to them in a way that they can comprehend.

Ravens are not as social as crows, you tend to see them alone, but they're confident, they are the smartest of all birds, and they have a reputation for solving complicated problems. Ravens look for food that's rich in nutrition to give them what they need to survive. During breeding season, ravens become acrobatic while flying and they do elaborate dances, diving and rolling. In other words, ravens get excited when they know it's time to come together and birth something.

Get excited and know that GOD has plans to birth something great out of you! After all, why else are you still here? Why have people around you died, but you're still here? You're here because you have an appointment with destiny.

My wife says, "Every morning when I wake up, I realize that GOD is not through with me yet." It's another day, another chance.

CHAPTER 1

The Pleasure of Pain and the Cost of My Anointing

Pain is not always bad; it causes you to produce. Most importantly it's an indication that after all you've been through, you're still here. It also tells you that in the midst of your affliction you haven't lost the ability to feel.

The intensity of pain is based on your perception; it's all about how you look at it.

Pain is not designed to kill you, but bring the best out of you. It is through pain that you find out who you really are.

Nothing can be birthed without pain. You overcome your pain by staying close to GOD. Praising GOD and worshipping GOD is the greatest resource you have in dealing with pain.

Praise and worship in the midst of pain declare that GOD is going to deliver me from the situation or he's going to deliver my mind in the midst of the situation.

Sometimes we stay in the fire a little longer because

before GOD changes "it" he has to change "us."

In order for the situation to change, we have to change, and in order for us to change, our mind has to change. When your mind changes, it's something that you will never have to go through again, and if you do, you know how to deal with it. When GOD changes your mind, he teaches you how to wait on him with the expectation that GOD is going to change this situation or he's going to change how you handle the situation.

Daniel's experience in the lion's den was amazing and prophetic. It reaches through generations to give us clarity and insight on how to go through our test.

Daniel was in the lion's den and the king was troubled all night; in the morning the king arose and went to the lion's den and asked Daniel a question:

"O Daniel, servant of the living GOD, is thy GOD whom thou servest continually able to deliver thee from the lions?"

Daniel responded that GOD had sent his angel and shut the lion's mouth. This text tells us that sometimes GOD will mute the situation before he delivers us from the situation. Your prayer should be "GOD, if it's not time for me to come out, shut the mouth of the lion."

There I was lying on the ground in excruciating pain. Every breath I took felt like someone was stabbing me in the stomach. It was a terrible accident. I didn't know what was going on in my body, but what I did know was that something was terribly wrong, I was eleven years old; it's been thirty-three years and I can still remember what that pain felt like.

My mother and father rushed me to St. Joe's Hospital, where the X-ray showed that my spleen had burst. At the time I had never heard the word "spleen" and I wasn't aware of its functions.

I would later find out that the spleen is an abdominal organ involved in the production and removal of blood cells in most vertebrates and forming part of the immune system. The spleen helps fight bacteria that cause pneumonia and meningitis.

I had what they call ruptured spleen, a life-threatening emergency because it can cause serious internal bleeding. The doctors told my parents that they had to get me into surgery immediately or it would be devastating.

At the time my dad was not a Christian; he made sure to get my mother and myself to church every week, but he did not attend. With tears rolling down his face, he walked down to the chapel and he told GOD, "If you heal my son, and allow him to live, I will give you my life for the rest of my life." Well, I'm still here, and my dad has faithfully served GOD for over thirty-three years and he's still going strong, serving GOD and taking care of the House of GOD where I serve as senior pastor.

I always love the fact that GOD used my injury to save my father and at the same time allowed my injury to be part of the price for my anointing. My dad is my hero. Just think about it—he gave up the world to make a covenant with GOD to save my life. If my dad never entered into that covenant with GOD, there's a great chance that I might not be here.

The doctor performed the surgery and GOD gave us success. After the surgery was complete the doctor made his way to find my parents in the waiting room. Not knowing what to expect, my parents listened very attentively to what the doctor had to say. It was apparent that something in that operating room had stunned them.

The doctor explained how long the surgery took, that I was doing fine, and then he said something happened that he had never seen before. While they were removing one spleen, they found another spleen inside of me. Human beings usually have one spleen, but they found that GOD had placed another spleen inside of me.

It was as if GOD was saying that he had an assignment for me and that he was going to make sure I had everything I needed to fulfill his purpose.

My mother often tells me a story about the first time the nurse placed me in her arms. She said she looked at me and knew that this child was special and GOD had something great for him to do. My mom knew it from that day, but others knew it when the doctor revealed that GOD had given me double.

Destiny is a direct result of your decision making. In other words, destiny is created based on what decisions you will make later in life. I believe one of the reasons that my life was spared is because GOD knew that I would say yes to his will and his plan for my life.

I often wonder if some people don't make it because

GOD is fully aware that they will never submit to his will. It's almost like I feel GOD saying, "If I give you a second chance to live, what are you going to do with it? I'm not going to save you for you to go back. If I save you, I'm saving you because I know that you're going to pursue the purpose that I have for your life. I want you to understand that your ability to say yes to GOD may be the very thing that spares your life.

I owe GOD. Anything he wants, I say yes. GOD has been so good to me, I want him to always know that he can have confidence that I will do whatever he asks. My favorite saying is "You don't know like I know what the Lord has done for me."

This relationship that I have with GOD is filled with victories, mercy, grace, secrets, unspoken battles, things that I can't share with anyone but GOD. He's been there through it all. He's loved me, corrected me, taught me, and tremendously blessed me. I can't even imagine my life without GOD. I think my favorite things that I share with GOD are my secrets.

I love the fact that I can be myself with GOD. I can tell him anything and he won't judge me for speaking the truth. I love the fact that he can handle my transparency. When JESUS dealt with the woman at the well, he sent his disciples away to the city to purchase food. He did this because he wanted to give the woman a private deliverance. Everybody can't be present for your deliverance; they can't handle what GOD is going to pull out of you.

The reason I know that JESUS wanted to give her a

private deliverance is because when the disciples returned with the meat, JESUS didn't even eat. Why would he send them to buy food if he wasn't going to eat it?

He knew that they wouldn't be able to handle the presence of her deliverance.

CHAPTER 2

Crazy Gets the Blessing

The word *crazy* is a word that we tend to stay away from because we have been taught that it means to be affected with madness, to become mentally deranged or obsessed. Crazy does in fact mean to be affected with madness, but crazy also means to deviate from proportion or moderation; it means to go from normal to abnormal; it means to go from logical to illogical.

In Isaiah 55:8 GOD tells us that his thoughts are not our thoughts; neither are our ways, his ways.

When you serve GOD success will come at the expense of people not understanding what GOD is telling you, and that's fine. What GOD shares with you is not for everybody to understand.

GOD will tell you something that logically just doesn't make sense.

In the 20th chapter of Numbers the children of Israel entered a desert called Zin, a place where there was no water.

The people began to scold and rebuke Moses.

Moses and Aaron left the presence of the people and went into the presence of GOD. The Lord told Moses, "Take your rod and gather the people together, speak to the rock before their eyes and water is going to flow out of the rock."

Moses, being frustrated because of the people and dealing with his own unbelief, hit the rock and the Bible says that water came out abundantly. Now GOD was offended, and the reason he was offended was because he told Moses to speak to the rock; he didn't tell him to hit the rock.

It is not Moses' frustration that offended GOD; it is not Moses' unbelief that offended GOD. It is the fact that Moses failed to sanctify GOD in the eyes of the children of Israel.

The Nation of Israel's faith would have increased intensely if he had spoken to the rock. Hitting the rock gave Moses glory; speaking to the rock would have given GOD the glory.

When GOD tells you to do something that doesn't make sense, he's setting something up so that he and only he can get the glory out of this.

If it makes sense, then people can get the glory. When it doesn't make sense, that indicates that GOD has moved all resources out of the way so that all the attention is pointed to him. You have to trust GOD even when you can't see your way out.

I started pastoring in August 2006, and my first sermon

was titled "Laugh Now, but You'll Praise Me Later." It came from the 18th chapter of Genesis where the Lord came to the earth and he visited Abraham and Sarah.

Before the Lord left he told Abraham, "Your wife is going to have a son." Abraham was ninety-nine years old and Sarah was eighty-nine years old when the Lord spoke this; the Bible says that Sarah laughed within herself. It wasn't a laugh that was vocal, but yet GOD heard her.

GOD asked Abraham, "Why is your wife laughing? Do you think there is anything that is hard for me to perform? I am a witness. GOD can do the impossible. I speak into your life that what makes you laugh will one day make you praise."

Like most men, I had some concern about my family's future. One particular evening I was sitting at a desk in my bedroom, my wife was asleep, and I started getting pop-ups about stock options and what the cost was per share. At the time I was not familiar with the procedures of the stock market, and as I sat there I heard a small voice say, *Invest in GOD's stock market.*

I increased my tithes from 10 percent to 20 percent, then 30 percent; there were times when I tithed 100 percent. I would give my entire check. I have seen blessings from GOD that I never dreamed of, and it unlocked a realm of favor in my life. Anything I asked GOD for, I received it. I started this in 2002; it's 2016 and I'm still reaping the harvest from investing in the tithing system.

About twelve years ago I heard GOD say, "You'll never be broke again," and let me tell you, he was right. Since

GOD spoke those words, I have been blessed with crazy blessings. During those years I kept hearing, "To get something crazy, you gotta do something crazy." I had no idea that GOD was about to show me what that really meant.

CHAPTER 3

The Release

In July 2002 my parents were taking a trip to Las Vegas and they invited me and my wife. I was a little apprehensive because I had heard that Las Vegas is a place that Christians shouldn't be. I had developed many misconceptions about Las Vegas from people who probably had never been themselves.

After we arrived, I immediately knew that I had been lied to. It was nowhere near what people had described. It was family oriented, with great shows and great food. I had the best time with my parents and with my wife. I often think about the great time I would have missed if I would have allowed man's traditions and misconceptions to prevent me from going on a family trip. Quite often, we miss out on special occasions with our family members because we allow people to tell us what's holy and what's not. Some moments you can never get back. Allow the Holy Ghost to direct you on what you should do and what you should not do.

On my return flight all I could think was *I can't wait to get home so that I can get to the gym and work off all this good eating.*

We got home on Monday evening. All of a sudden I had an overwhelming desire to go to the church that I was attending and pray. I had gone to the church on other occasions and prayed, so this wasn't anything new, but there was something different about this visit. I kept hearing the words "I'm going to see the king." I jumped in the shower, put on my favorite suit, got my cologne, and noticed that it was after 11:00 p.m. If my wife woke up and saw this, how would I explain this to her?

It didn't matter. I was on my way to see the King, and I knew I couldn't come to him any kind of way. I knew I couldn't come without a gift; like I said, this was a different night. I couldn't figure it out, but I knew I had to get to JESUS.

I didn't have a lot of money, but I had been keeping change in this huge apple juice jar. I still remember the jar; it was glass and it had a yellow label on the front. I grabbed it and I made my way to the house of GOD.

I arrived, walked in the church, and stood before the altar. I began to pray to GOD and call out to GOD like I never had before. I was thirsty for GOD. After prayer I poured all of the coins out of that jar, everything that I had, and I stood still and I heard GOD say, "I just released it." I didn't know what he had released but I knew I heard his voice.

I went home still enjoying the presence of GOD. I

drifted off to sleep with my mind on GOD; the best sleep is when you wind down your evening praying, reading the word of GOD and meditating on his goodness. Proverbs 3:24 says, "When you lay down, don't be afraid, your sleep shall be sweet."

CHAPTER 4

Basketball: The Teacher of Life

Tuesday July 23, 2002 is a day that I will remember for the rest of my life. I got my gym clothes together, and I went to the fitness center. I saw a couple of people on the basketball court and so I decided to play. The game of basketball has been a part of my life ever since I could remember.

As a little kid I would bend a hanger and slide it in between the top of my door and shut the door. I would take paper, roll it up, and put masking tape on it to use as my basketball and I would shoot and work on my game. And then one day I discovered that we could purchase a Nerf hoop and I asked my mother to purchase one for me and she did. I was so excited. I'm amazed when I look back over my life and I remember how little things made me happy. I didn't ask for much. I just wanted to play basketball and play my musical instruments.

My cousin Jarrett Perdue would come over and we would play basketball in my house and we felt like we were actually on the hardwood playing full court, and then we would go in the basement and recreate martial art films that we had watched.

The little things made us happy; we didn't need much. We didn't have anything close to the technology that the kids have today, and we never used the word "bored." We were too creative to be bored.

My mother and my father were very protective. As a little boy they didn't allow me to go wherever I wanted, and at the time I didn't understand it. But now that I'm older I thank GOD that they were protective, because it wasn't so much about protecting me; it was more about protecting my purpose, my calling, my destiny.

I wish more parents would understand that GOD is holding them accountable to protect their children, because in protecting the child, you're protecting their future, their destiny, their purpose—you're protecting the reason GOD created them.

When I asked to go outside, my parents would let me but I had to stay in front of the house. My friends had basketball hoops on their garage, but I couldn't get to them. The love I had for basketball was so strong that I used an open branch on the tree in front of our house as a basketball rim, and what's crazy is, I was able to convince my friends who had basketball hoops to come to my house and play with me.

When I look back at this, I realize that the gift of leadership was in me even then, because I was able to convince people to leave a real hoop and come play on a branch that

I was using as a hoop, and make it so entertaining for them that they didn't miss what they gave up.

Basketball has been very therapeutic for me; it has always been a stress reliever. When I'm going through something, I can go play ball and it takes my mind completely off of whatever it is that I'm dealing with. It also has ignited a competitiveness inside me that drives me in every area of my life. In basketball I've always wanted to win so bad, I've played in pain, I've defended the best player, and even today at forty-three years old, I will defend a person who is hitting shots or posting up. These kids are bigger, faster, stronger, but my will to win makes me overlook attributes.

I've always had this chip on my shoulder that I wanted to be known as the best, and I always want to win in everything. I'm mad when I lose. I don't like to lose in board games, card games, nothing. I don't like to lose when I know that I can win. I never got that "sore loser" talk—who made that up anyway? I'm not supposed to be happy that I lose. GOD created us to win.

My friends Brian, Wendell, and Lori have woken me up at midnight talking trash, and I got out of my bed and went to the court and we would sometimes play until 2:00 a.m. because I have a competitive appetite that is never filled.

The competitiveness that I have for basketball has been a driving force in other areas of my life, and I take that same competitive edge into preaching. I don't compete with other preachers, but I have a drive that makes me prepare each sermon and give the best presentation that I can.

Sometimes GOD gives me my sermon at the last

minute, because he knows that I have such a competitive drive to be the best and show people that I'm the best that sometimes I over study and I over prepare. I have to learn to discipline myself. Sometimes GOD doesn't want a sermon to be deep, sometimes he wants just a basic message, but I have a hard time with basic, mainly because I feel it's a sin to be good when GOD called you to be great.

Basketball has been such a great teacher in my life. I've learned many lessons about life through basketball; for instance, you don't always have to take the last shot. Sometimes you may have to set a pick for the shooter and let someone else take the last shot. I apply lessons like that to life. It's not always about you. There are times when you have to do some work and help the next person shine.

My mentality is not how many shots I can take; it's about doing whatever I have to do to win. If I have to grab the rebounds of life, that's fine. If I have to give the assist of life, that's fine too. I just want to win. Whatever I have to do to win in life, I'll do it.

My coaches have been, as they say, a blessin' and lesson.

I was in the fourth grade, playing for my school team, and we were dominating other teams, but one day we ran into the Richland Eagles. The team was led by a kid named Bryan Allen, who is now Bishop Bryan Allen, and they beat us bad. I mean, everything we tried to do they countered it. My coach called a timeout and started cursing at us. Now remember, we were in the fourth grade so we were probably nine years old. He looked at me and said, "Are you going to keep letting them kick your a** or are you going to do something about it?" I hit the bench and I got up and I gave it my all on the court. We didn't win, but that day ignited a competitiveness that would be with me forever.

After that I had coaches who taught me discipline and allowed me to use my gift on the basketball court, but it was the summer that led into my junior year that would change the course of my life.

The varsity coach called me into his office and said, "Deon, you won't be able to suit up for games this year, but I want you to participate in practice every day. If you prove yourself then you can suit up your senior year."

I was devastated, but I kept my composure. What I didn't realize then was that he was using me, allowing me to participate in practice but not games; allowing me to help get the guys ready that he wanted to play. In practice I was always on the other team. I played the part of the team members we had scouted to help us prepare for the games.

It was a devastating blow for my coach to tell me that I wouldn't play in any games but I had to practice every day. Every day during practice I made somebody pay, blocking shots, taking the ball away, trying to dunk on somebody. I was upset, but I wasn't going to give up. I wanted to show the coach that he made a mistake. I was embarrassed. I told my parents not to come to the games.

I didn't finish the season out because my father took me off the team—not because of what the coach did to me, but because I had messed up the side of his car trying to back it out of the garage to go see a girl.

I always wondered why he didn't get more angry about that situation until I was telling this story during one of my sermons. Afterward he told me he wasn't aware that I was going to see a girl; he thought I was just trying to get to school. We laugh about it now, but it wasn't funny when it happened.

CHAPTER 5

He Did It on Purpose

Tuesday July 23, 2002 is a day that I will remember for the rest of my life: it was the day after I went to the church to pray and give GOD my gift. I got my gym clothes together, and I went to the fitness center. I saw a couple of people on the basketball court and so I decided to play.

We opened up with a game of 32, every man for himself, and then we decided to pick teams and run a full-court game. I noticed an employee of the fitness center come in and join the game, although at the time he was on the clock and supposed to be working. We ran up and down the court a few times and then the unimaginable happened. The employee, a man who is 6'4" and around 280 pounds, grabbed a rebound and swung his elbows back and forth appearing to keep people from taking the ball from him. When he swung his elbows, he hit me in the face, particularly the eye area.

Being in an enormous amount of pain, I put my hand

to my face and I fell to the ground. One of the participants helped me find a seat. The pain was excruciating, but what made me afraid was the fact that I couldn't see out of my left eye.

While all of this was going on, the employee recruited a guy from the sideline and returned to playing basketball, never offering me any assistance. He did not check on me; he never went to the front desk to report what happened. He continued to play basketball. After a while my vision started to return but it was blurred. I made my way up to the front desk, told them what had transpired, and I asked if I could use the phone to call my wife to come and get me.

We went to the emergency room at Silver Cross Hospital, where the doctor examined me and sent me to get X-rays. The nurse brought me back to the room, and my wife and I patiently waited for the results. The door opened and the doctor approached. At that time I was thinking he was going to give me medicine for pain and send me home.

I was totally wrong. Dr. Russell informed me that my orbit bone on my left eye was fractured, my nose was fractured, there was discharge in the left eye, and he noticed that there was some tearing in the left eye. On top of that he diagnosed me having an inflamed conjunctiva, meaning that my eyelids were swollen. During the examination he also found mucosal thickening involving the left maxillary sinus.

I was shocked and I couldn't believe that this was happening to me. I remember thinking, *I just went to the church last night and spent time with GOD and gave him all the money I had left. How could this happen?*

Dr. Russell gave me a referral for a specialist because my injuries were severe; as a result of this injury I started to develop severe headaches. The eye specialist reported that my vision had gotten worse, and believed that this was one of the contributing factors to my headaches. I became concerned when the doctors told me to monitor my eyeball to make sure that it didn't start to sink. They told me if the eyeball sank, surgery would be needed, and if they performed the surgery there was a great possibility that I could lose my sight as a result.

I was devastated. I felt like GOD had abandoned me. Here I was living holy, being faithful to GOD, serving GOD, not slippin and dippin but saved for real, and the doctor told me that an injury from a simple game of recreation basketball had left me with the possibility that my eyeball could sink and I could possibly lose my eyesight.

On top of this, I started having problems breathing; the doctor informed me that this was the result of my nose being fractured and having a septal deflection. Out of all the injuries, the severe headaches affected me the most; there were times when I could do nothing but sit still and wait for the headache to leave. Sometimes it took minutes, sometimes it took hours. It's been fourteen years and I still suffer with those headaches. I thank GOD for grace—the headaches are not as bad as they used to be, and they are not as frequent as they once were.

For a while I suffered with double vision, and the doctors advised me not to participate in sports anymore. They gave me a poor prognosis and told me that I would simply have to learn to live with my discomforts for the rest of my life.

All five of my doctors gave a clinical opinion within a great degree of medical certainty, that my injuries were a direct result of the incident on July 23, 2002 and that they were permanent.

I didn't understand it then, but now I see that GOD did it on purpose. To accomplish his plan sometimes GOD will allow things—not cause, but allow things—to happen in our life, and we don't understand why. Two things are happening: he wants you to move from good to greater, or he wants to get the glory, or both. One of my favorite scriptures is 1st Peter 4:12. "Beloved think it not strange concerning the fiery trial which is to try you, as though some strange thing happened unto you: but rejoice, inasmuch as ye are partakers of Christ's sufferings; that, when his glory shall be revealed, ye may be glad also with exceeding joy."

This scripture is telling you to get excited about trials in your life that you did not bring on yourself, because what you're going through, you're going through for GOD to get the glory out of it. But because you had to go through it, GOD is going to compensate you for it.

I love the part that says that after the glory is revealed, you're going to be glad with exceeding joy. That tells us GOD is going to exceed that which normally brings you the greatest joy and pleasure.

We think we know what brings us joy, but GOD knows what really will make and keep us happy.

CHAPTER 6

I Need a Lawyer

Soon my medical bills began to come in. I wasn't able to work, but I thank GOD for my wife. She graduated from college and has been a government employee for twenty-five years now; she started working for the government when she was in high school.

This woman was created in the throne room, I'm sure. When GOD gave her to me, he gave me everything that I would ever need. Before anyone heard me preach she was my first audience; since day one, she has always pushed me to pursue my dreams. She believes in me, she's my filter, and she keeps me balanced, constantly telling me, "D, don't be harsh on them. D, don't deal with that today. D, don't address that right now; we're at a baby shower."

I love her so much, and I work hard to give her the world. She has a brilliant mind, but simple desires; a creative genius, she's a true go-getter, but she has a way of making me feel like she needs me when she really doesn't. GOD groomed her well.

She held down the house and paid the bills, but as a man I couldn't feel comfortable letting her handle all the weight. I began to contact lawyers. A few of them listened to my story but later refused the case. Some lawyers wouldn't allow me to give them the details; they flat-out said they weren't interested in taking the case.

Finally I made contact with a successful lawyer in Chicago, and we met and I gave him the details of my injury. He agreed to take the case. I was relieved because after being rejected by so many lawyers I was afraid that this well-known fitness center would get off the hook and not be held accountable for the actions of their employee.

Weeks went by and I didn't hear anything from the attorney, so I would call and get the runaround. Sometimes my calls would be ignored, and my request for a return phone call would be denied.

One day I went to the mail and I noticed an envelope from the law firm. For a few seconds I was happy because they were finally contacting me, but my joy quickly left when I opened the letter and read that they would no longer represent me. No explanation, nothing. I was crushed. I was thinking, *All this wasted time. You didn't have the heart to tell me this on the phone but you sent it in a letter*. I was upset and I wanted an explanation.

I called the firm and I asked to speak to the attorney. When he got on the phone I was respectful and I asked him why he changed his mind and declined to represent me. He informed me that when I had joined this fitness center, I signed a waiver that prevented me from pursuing litigation because of personal injury and that I had no case.

I said okay, thank you, and I hung up the phone. I was hurt and disappointed. I called my wife and she assured me that GOD was still going to work this out.

One evening I was in the car by myself driving to Bible study. I love my jazz station, but for some reason I decided to turn the radio to the Christian station. There was an attorney giving advice concerning law. Normally I wouldn't have kept that station on because of the subject matter, but for some reason I couldn't turn it off. In a matter of minutes, a person called in to the show and asked the attorney if he had ever heard of a person representing themselves.

The lawyer responded that yes he had heard of it, and he began to deal with the pros and cons of representing yourself in court. I was sitting in the church parking lot but I couldn't finish listening to the show because my pastor was expecting me to be on time. I got out of my car and I headed into service. My body was there, but my mind was miles away. All I could think about was representing myself, and I wondered if GOD had allowed me to hear that program for a reason.

After our pastor dismissed Bible study I couldn't wait to get in the car and call my wife and tell her about my new revelation. I called her from my cell phone, and I said, "Babe, I think GOD wants me to represent myself in court." Being the supportive wife that she is, she said, "Okay, let me know if there's anything I can do."

Immediately I began my research. I spent hours upon

hours reading and learning how to put a lawsuit together, what format to use. I wanted to make sure that I used the correct words. GOD has always taught me to operate in the spirit of excellence, and I wanted to make sure that I offered the best presentation I could. The Internet was very helpful. I also spent time at the law library, and I was able to view examples of other personal injury lawsuits that had been filed.

I started researching personal injury lawsuits and found out that some lawsuits are won simply by being able to reference another case similar to yours.

The church that I was attending belonged to an organization, and we would often come together with other churches that were in the same organization. One evening I was sitting in the service and a pastor got up to raise an offering. Before he could get to his assignment, he began to prophesy. I don't remember everything that he said, but what I will never forget is, he said, "GOD gave you favor in the courtroom." He did not say it directly to me, but he released it in the atmosphere and I grabbed it. I've always been intrigued by the fact that GOD didn't give me that word before I started the process for my suit, but the word came after I started the process.

This is how GOD works. Confirmation does not always come before you make a move; sometimes the confirmation will come after you've made the move, because making the move before the confirmation indicates that you have faith.

In the 12th chapter of Genesis GOD tells Abraham to leave his country, his kindred, and to leave his father's house and "go to a land that I will show you." GOD is telling him to move, "even though you don't know where I'm taking you. I want you to move, and later I'll tell you where you're going, but right now, I need your faith to increase."

I often correct people about praying for their faith to increase. Praying for your faith to increase is similar to praying for patience—never pray for patience. When you pray for your faith to increase or for patience you're basically asking GOD to take you through.

The only way for GOD to give you patience is to take you through a horrific situation where you're in it for a period of time and you have no other choice but to wait for GOD to bring you out.

Don't pray for patience. It doesn't have to be given; patience can be acquired. How? By learning to wait on GOD, your experience can teach you patience.

I felt an extra boost from the Word I received that night. When I returned home I proceeded in my research, and after weeks of preparation I put my lawsuit together and I went to the courthouse. I asked the clerk what was needed to file the suit. I was excited and nervous at the same time.

The clerk informed me what was needed to complete the process. I was relieved because I had everything that she requested, and then she told me that it would be two hundred dollars to file. Now, two hundred dollars doesn't sound bad, but at the time I was not able to work and I didn't have a lot of money.

I went home discouraged. I couldn't believe all the hard work I'd accomplished was being halted because of two hundred dollars. My wife asked how things went, I told her, and her response was "Don't worry about the money, baby. I got it for you."

That moment really defined who I was married to; she was willing to invest in an assignment that GOD had given me.

I filed the lawsuit and I waited for a response from the defendant's attorney. In the back of my mind, I was hoping that they would receive the lawsuit and settle quickly. I felt that I wasn't able to take this case to trial and battle a team of professionally trained lawyers. Instead they filed a reply in support of motion to dismiss.

I received a notice that informed me of our first court date. GOD had given me instruction to wear a suit with a sharp tie, not bright colors, but a suit with a soft tone, black or dark blue. Every time I went to court I wore a dark suit with a sharp tie. I was dressed so well that some of the attorneys thought I was a lawyer.

The concept that GOD gave me has helped me even until this very day. If I go to the doctor's office, or if I had to go to my children's school, I wore a suit. Perception is everything; people perceive you based on how you present yourself.

Going to your children's school in a suit tells the teacher, *You're dealing with a child who is about something; give them the best attention and the best care.* It shouldn't be like that but this is the world we live in.

My first day in court was a little intimidating. When I entered the room there were only a couple of lawyers present. I was informed that you have to check in, so I checked in and found a seat. I looked around the room, wondering if my opponent had arrived yet.

My stomach was full of butterflies. I was nervous. I had dreamed of this day but to actually be here, on this big stage, I felt out of place. These men and women invested years in law school, countless hours of studying, sitting in courtrooms observing other lawyers; they tried many cases and had years of experience. Here I was with no experience in law. I was concerned with what those lawyers were thinking about me. Did they take me seriously? Did they know that I wasn't a lawyer? What if I said the wrong thing?

By 9 a.m. the room was full of attorneys. I was the only one there representing myself. On cue, the bailiff said, "All rise" and he introduced the judge who was in charge. I waited patiently as the clerk called each case, and just as I finally became relaxed, I heard a voice call for my case.

I stood up, squared my shoulders together, raised my head up, and approached the judge. The attorney for the defendant told the judge that we were here for a personal injury suit filed by Mr. Hayes. I froze. I didn't say anything, because I didn't know what to say; my opponent did all the talking that first day. This was all new to me. I had everything planned out in my head how the scenario would work, and it went nothing like I had daydreamed.

The attorney for the defendant asked the judge for time to reply to this lawsuit and the judge granted his request. We left the courtroom at separate times; my opponent took the stairs and I took the elevator.

When I exited the elevator, the attorney was waiting for

me. He looked me in my face, and he told me that my lawsuit was frivolous. I laughed and I told him, "You can't beat me, because GOD is with me."

There I was, not educated in law, telling a lawyer who was educated in law and had successfully won many lawsuits that he couldn't beat me because GOD was with me. For someone who is oblivious to the power of GOD, this may have seemed arrogant. This statement was not made out of arrogance, but based on the fact that when you trust GOD, when you are obedient, when you live the way that the Bible says, you will win every time. Psalm 37:34 says "Wait on the Lord, and keep his way, and he shall exalt thee to inherit the land: when the wicked are cut off, thou shalt see it."

The defendant's lawyer responded, I answered his response, and the judge told me that my lawsuit needed to be amended. In my mind it stated all the necessary information to successfully prove my case, but I went back home and amended my lawsuit. It took weeks of research, and it was very frustrating, because I felt that the judge rejected my argument, and now I had to come up with a different strategy.

I worked very hard gathering information, taking witness statements, proving a pattern of behavior, proving negligence on behalf of the employee, and each time I came back to court the judge would tell me that my suit needed to be amended. I felt as if the court was fighting against me; the proof that I needed was right in front of the judge's eyes. I felt that I had successfully proven my case, but my efforts had not yet brought me success.

The next year and a half would be an ongoing chess match. I would file my answer and the defendant's lawyer would file his response; we went back and forth. It was physically and mentally draining; sometimes I would wonder, Why would GOD give me a task if it wasn't going to bring immediate success?

Months of strange cars outside my apartment, following my wife and me, trying to discourage me and prompt me to rescind the lawsuit. It became frustrating. I even had concerns about my family's safety because of this lawsuit, but I was not about to give up. I was determined to make it to the finish line, no matter what obstacles came my way. I knew that I could overcome anything because GOD was with me. When I feel like someone is trying to intimidate me, I really come out swinging. The more you tell me that I can't do it, the more I'm motivated to prove that I *can* do it.

My opponent tried desperately to have my lawsuit dismissed, but every move he made, GOD was whispering in my ear and he showed me how to counter it. The Lord would speak to me the night before court and prepare me for some statements and how to counter what was going to be said. I look back on this case, and I remember how the first couple of times that we went to court, I was quiet, and when I would get in the car, I would be upset with myself that I didn't speak up and say more. Each time I made up in my mind that the next court date I would lose the nervous feelings and speak up. As the court dates went on, I began to speak up, and when I spoke up, the judge began to talk back to me as if I were a lawyer. It felt good and it gave me the courage to continue to speak up and not let my opponent dominate the conversation. At first I had a feeling that I wasn't allowed to talk because I was not an attorney. No one told me this; it was just a feeling that I had. GOD revealed to me that I had every right to speak, because I wasn't speaking on my behalf. I was speaking on the behalf of GOD.

The opposing lawyers became concerned because they thought that this lawsuit would be dismissed by now; they didn't expect me to get this far. They were losing, and they reached for the ace of spades that they had been holding onto.

The case took a turn when the defendant's lawyer brought to the judge that my lawsuit should be dismissed because I had signed a waiver when I joined the fitness center. The enemy tried to discourage me. I had made it this far, and I thought the waiver was far behind me and that it wouldn't be brought up again. I was wrong, but GOD gave me favor with the judge.

CHAPTER 7

Favor with the Judge

The judge looked at me and she said, "I can't give you the answer to help you over this hurdle, but do your research about waivers." I left the courtroom, I prayed, and I asked GOD to help me. I began to study about waivers concerning personal injury, and GOD led me to discover a term that I had never heard before: *willful and wanton conduct*. It means having previous knowledge of potential danger and failing to act.

GOD led me to understand that a company cannot have previous knowledge of an employee who has hurt people before, then hurt someone and hide behind a waiver. A waiver does not condone negligence.

Every pastor who reads this book, I want you to understand that willful and wanton conduct is not just for companies. GOD wants this to apply to the church as well. When you have a person in position and they are hurting people, you have to deal with them. It doesn't matter how gifted they are, how much they tithe, how influential they are—you can't be afraid of confrontation at the expense of people being hurt.

In my ten years of pastoring, I found that gifted people intimidate other gifted people. In church we have a feeling of entitlement, that *something belongs to me*, or *That's my song. I didn't write it, but I'm the only one who can sing it.* Church people are territorial, because church is the only place where I can become what I couldn't become in the world.

This is why I teach our church members to have a life outside of church. When you don't have a life outside of church, you become possessive about title and positions because "this is all I got." You become intimidated when GOD sends someone who is just as gifted as you are or can do the job better than you can. Insecure people need to be needed, so they don't like people who can make the show go on without them.

I've had to move people out of positions because they were possessive about their assignment. Possessive emotions will make you hurt other people, and when this happens, the leader must confront this or risk the possibility of an implosion.

Pastors, GOD is holding you accountable. If you have previous knowledge of potential danger and you fail to act, GOD is going to hold you responsible. Every person you allowed to be run off, every person you allowed to be hurt, you're going to have to give an account for them.

And if you don't move that toxic person, he or she will

tear your church up. The bad thing about the toxic person is that they never admit when they're wrong, and the people who know they're wrong enable them to continue wrong by not confronting their wrong. Proverbs 27:6 says, "Faithful are the wounds of a friend; but the kisses of an enemy are deceitful."

It's better for someone close to you to wound you by telling you the truth. A person who knows that you're wrong and won't tell you is really an enemy.

I amended my lawsuit and this time I filed it based on willful and wanton conduct.

I knew I had got them this time. I was sure to win my case. I was thinking that they probably would settle out of court because through the help of GOD, we had taken away all of their resources for them to fight. There was no way they could beat this willful and wanton conduct.

Through my investigations I had found that other participants had been injured by this same employee. I also found out that there were occasions when parents were present when their children were hurt by this same employee and they reported it to the fitness center. I took depositions from parents and other participants who had been injured by this employee. I had no idea that he had hurt this many people.

Upon further investigation I found out that an employee at the front desk had witnessed the employee injure participants, and this was all the evidence I needed to prove that the defendant had previous knowledge of potential danger and failed to act. Not only did this popular fitness center allow the employee to continue to work for them, but they also allowed him to continue to play basketball with other participants while he was working. Even after my injury, they still allowed him to work there and play basketball with the members.

I sent out subpoenas to other witnesses and I conducted my own deposition. I was also present for the deposition conducted by the defendant.

There was one particular deposition that I will hold near to my heart forever. The opposing attorney scheduled a deposition for my witness, and I arrived early that morning. I walked into the room and met a nice lady who was full of energy, and when I mentioned GOD, she couldn't stop talking about him; it was clear that she had an intense relationship with GOD. She told me her name was Bernice Betts and she explained that she was appointed by the court to take notes of this deposition. I was so comfortable in this deposition because a woman of GOD was in the room with us.

I objected and accused the attorney of leading the witness. I was using all types of lawyer vernacular. At the end of the deposition Mrs. Bernice told me how proud of me she was, and that she was really impressed how I handled myself. Her favorite part was when I told the opposing lawyer that he was "leading the witness."

I was so honored that GOD put a Christian woman on this particular case; it was just another sign that GOD was with me. Years later when I started pastoring, I looked up and couldn't believe my eyes—Bernice was standing in my church.

She visited a couple of times, but her last visit is the one that I will never forget. Every first Saturday of the month we have 6 a.m. prayer, and as prayer concluded I played the keyboard and she danced like she was dancing for GOD.

She moved with grace and she truly danced like no one was watching. I had no idea that this would be the last time I would see her. She passed and made her way into eternity. I'm so glad that I was able to meet her and I will forever cherish those moments of how GOD connected her to my assignment for a short time.

Effectiveness is not based on how long you know a person, but the impact you make with the time you have with a person.

CHAPTER 8

I Need an Alternate Ending

The depositions had been completed, our next court date was quickly approaching, and I was overjoyed. I knew the day that I had dreamed about was almost here. I prayed and I fasted and I declared victory. Finally the day arrived, and I woke up early. I couldn't sleep because of the excitement I felt. I knew this was it. I played different scenarios in my mind how the case was going to end that day and what my response was going to be. I even daydreamed about what gift I would purchase for my wife with my settlement money and what I would do for my parents.

I arrived at court almost forty-five minutes early. I was excited that what GOD had promised me was about to manifest. I waited patiently for the clerk to call my case, and as soon as I heard the name Hayes, I immediately got up and stood before the judge. The judge looked at my amended suit with my witness statements, all of my paperwork was in order, and she said, "I'm dismissing your lawsuit." I couldn't believe it. My heart dropped. I was stunned. I was just trying to keep it together in front of all these lawyers and the judge. I did my best to hold back my tears, but it literally felt like the breath had been taken out of my body. I had never been that hurt before in my life.

I left the courtroom. It was a Friday morning, and the city had started an event called Marketplace Friday. The streets were filled with people, some who knew me, and to get to my car I had to go through the marketplace. I lost it. I don't ever remember crying like that. I heard someone call my name, but I couldn't even look back. I made it to my car and I broke down real bad. It was the first time ever in my life that I cried to the point where I couldn't breathe.

I called my wife and told her what happened. I was crying so bad she couldn't understand what I was saying. I was truly hurt; it was the worst feeling I ever had in my life. I had trusted GOD and I felt that he had left me; if felt like all my hard work was done in vain. *GOD, how could you allow this to happen? Did I hear you wrong?* I couldn't make sense of it.

My wife left work to come home because she was worried about me, and it was hard to look her in the face. I had told her GOD told me to do this, but now I had to deal with the reality that I had lost. GOD had used me to prophesy to other people, but now the word that I spoke on my own life seemed to not have any life. I had a fear that my wife would lose faith in my gift. I didn't understand it. I was used to GOD saying yes, but now I had to feel the agony of No. It took some time to get through the initial shock of what happened, but GOD began to deal with me, and I would hear a small voice say, *It's not over.*

At this particular time, the movie industry was selling DVDs with alternate endings; if you didn't like the way that a movie ended, you selected the option button on your remote control and pressed "alternate endings," and this is how GOD began to show me my life. If I don't like how things are going, pray and ask GOD for an alternate ending. I felt this with my lawsuit. Although the judge had dismissed my case, something told me that GOD was about to give me an alternate ending.

I have to stop and speak into your life. Don't be afraid or discouraged when things don't work out the way you anticipate. You have to find the good in good-bye and ignore the hell in hello. Let go of what GOD tells you has exceeded time in your life, and ignore the hell in hello by not being afraid to start over again. You may have been knocked down, but somehow you have got to reach deep and pull out the tenacity to get up and try this thing again. Because GOD said it's going to work, you have to trust the process, and the process may mean hearing twelve no's before you hear one yes.

After weeks of processing what happened, I learned that my cousin was dating a woman who happened to be paralegal. I was introduced to her and I explained what transpired and I asked her what I could do. She told me that I needed to file an appeal, and she would help me. I gave her all of my files, notes, research, witness statements—anything involving the case, I gave it to her.

After a couple of weeks, she disappeared. Her phone was disconnected, and the place she was living was now vacant. I exhausted every option to get in touch with her. I never heard from her again; even unto this day I haven't heard from her. I was worried. I was concerned about her, but I also was concerned because she had everything that pertained to my lawsuit. All my hard work was gone, my research, my statements, my records, all gone.

We filed the appeal, and I said, "GOD, it's in your hands. I don't have any of my paperwork, I don't know where this woman is, but Lord, I trust you, I believe."

Remember, faith is belief that does not rest on logical proof or material evidence.

Faith is a confidence or trust. Faith is a bold proclamation of what GOD can do. Faith is confidence that GOD will do what he has promised to do.

Once again, I spoke to my wife, and I told her, "I'm going to win. I know the judge dismissed my case, but GOD promised me victory in the courtroom." No matter how many times life knocks you down, no matter how many disappointments you face, you cannot let it eradicate your faith.

In the 2nd chapter of Genesis it tells us that a river went out of Eden to water the garden, and from there it split into four heads; one river flowed to a land called Havilah, where there was gold, bdellium, and the onyx stone. Adam and Eve missed it because they were so focused on the tree. When we focus on what we can't do, we miss what we can do. The tree introduced them to sin, but the four river flow would have introduced them to resources and prosperity.

It wasn't my assignment to focus on what the judge said, but to remember what GOD said. If GOD says he's going to do it, he will do it; there is no way he can fail. Nothing can stop him.

CHAPTER 9

I Ordained the Struggle

My pastor decided it was time for him to retire. His tenure as pastor was short, and I didn't understand his decision. I didn't want him to leave. I wanted him to stay and I had prayed that he would change his mind, but I had a dream in which I saw him leaving so I knew that destiny was already set.

My mother was the assistant pastor, and she did an amazing job in bringing structure to the administrative side, but there were people who fought against her because they wanted to select their own pastor. My mom is an amazing preacher and teacher, but most importantly she is an amazing administrator. A lot of the success of my church, One Vision Worship Center, is attributed to the organization of the administrative office that my mother has structured. My mom taught me structure, she taught me foundation, she taught me how to love people, she taught me how to preach love to GOD's people, and she taught me how to encourage the people through sermons and not beat them down.

I get irritated when I hear a preacher beating people down over the pulpit. There are certain preachers I can't listen to because they sound angry, they sound bitter, they sound like they're nagging. People don't come to church to be judged or verbally abused, nor do they come to be reminded that they're sinners. We know that. We need you to tell us how to get out of this.

When my pastor left, my mother was attacked by church folks because they felt they knew who would make the best pastor. It's hard to be still while people are attacking your loved ones, but we must remember that no one can protect them like GOD can. The funny thing is, my mother didn't even want the church; we had just got in a new building, and she wanted to protect the finances and increase them so that we would be able to maintain the building.

Finally our bishop came to her, and he told her that she was doing an awesome job; he said he didn't want to see her attacked anymore by the people, and he suggested that she allow him to bring in a pastor from the outside. Immediately my mother agreed. One evening, the bishop came to our church, turned to me, and said that GOD showed me to him in a dream. He also mentioned that one day I would pastor. I knew GOD had called me, at times I wasn't sure, but that moment awakened something in me that I was on the right track. But it wasn't time yet.

Timing is everything. We can have the right calling but the wrong timing. You can even have the right anointing but the wrong timing.

In the beginning I got along well with our new pastor. I was always respectful of him, I never crossed the line, I served him, and I protected him. We had a great relationship; he was the pastor, and I was his minister of music, for free! I often look back at that time and it amazes me how I was faithful in ministry. I taught Sunday school, helped cleaned the church, and played the organ for free.

I never even thought about asking my church to pay me, but yet I was faithful, on time, and on my post. They never had to wonder where I was. I was faithful to my assignment, and I was faithful to my pastor. I served in any capacity that I was needed in the church.

The week leading up to Thanksgiving 2005 was a life-changing event in my life.

We were supposed to have choir rehearsal early in the week, but I canceled the rehearsal because I had to pick my son up from his basketball game out of town and I knew that I wouldn't be able to make it back in time to rehearse.

The pastor called and asked me if I canceled rehearsal, and I said yes. He asked me why and I told him because I had to pick my son up from basketball and I knew that I would not be able to get back in time.

He went on this chastising rant and I said, "Pastor, respectfully, I didn't know that I was supposed to call you to cancel the rehearsal." There was a long silence on his end, and so I felt that he must have been offended by what I said. I apologized and he said okay.

Thanksgiving morning arrived. I got up early and prepared for our early morning service. I played the organ for the entire service, and after the service concluded, the pastor wanted to see me in his office, where he told me that he was sitting me down from all of my responsibilities.

He told me that I couldn't teach Sunday school, I couldn't testify, I couldn't preach at my home church, nor take any preaching engagements outside the church, and then he said I was not allowed to play the organ anymore. I asked him why and he said, "You lied about canceling choir rehearsal."

I said, "I didn't lie. Remember I told you that I canceled it?" At this time, I noticed that not once had he looked me in my face; for the entire conversation he couldn't look at me. "I did tell you that I canceled choir rehearsal. If I would have said no, then why did I go into the part about me canceling it to pick my son up from basketball?"

At this moment I had lost all respect for him because I knew he was lying. I believe he was upset because in our phone conversation when I had stated that I didn't know that I was supposed to call him in order to cancel the rehearsal, I wasn't disrespectful, but he didn't like what I had said and he had made up in his mind that he was going to show me who the boss was. I was very angry because I knew that this man was being used by Satan. In that office I had lost respect for him. I had never seen a pastor intentionally lie just to accomplish a mission. I told the pastor, "You know I didn't do this, but it's okay because GOD got me."

I couldn't believe that this pastor created a lie just to move me out of a position. I laugh now when I think about the fact that he stopped me from playing the organ, a position that I was a volunteer for. Why would I have to lie for a position that I'm not even getting paid for? I wasn't hurt, I was mad. I was mad because he lied and I was mad because he waited to do this on Thanksgiving. The entire holiday was messed up. My sisters were hurt, my mom was hurt, my father was mad. An entire holiday disrupted because of one evil man. I was also mad because out of all the people in that church who knew me and watched me grow up, none of them stood up for me, not one. Only my father stood up for me, and he let the pastor know that he would not be a part of what he was trying to do to me, not because I was his son, but because he knew that I was GOD'S anointed.

The next weekend came and I showed up to church. The pastor went into his office as if he was shocked and told the ministers that I was in the audience. He thought I was going to run, but one thing that my father taught me was to never run from anything, especially when you haven't done anything wrong.

I sat in the front row. I didn't sit in the front to be disrespectful, but my thought was, you sit in the back row when you're wrong and when you're embarrassed because of sin. I wanted to see how this pastor could lie and still preach. Every Sunday he preached about me, his sermons were all directed at me, and I sat there and I took it, still praising and worshiping GOD in the face of the devil. Man can take things from you, but one thing that no one can take is your ability to praise and worship GOD.

In the 137th Psalm the Babylonians had taken Jerusalem

captive. The scripture says that after they had been taken captive, they hung their harps upon the willows; in other words, they hung their instruments on the trees. I want to give you a word right now: never allow anyone to afflict you to the point where you want to put your gift up.

The captives told them, "Sing us one of the songs of Zion." Sometimes the beauty of this text is missed. People focus on the fourth verse where it says, "How can we sing the Lord's song in a strange land," but the prophecy of the text is the Babylonians' request for a "song of Zion." The songs of Zion were songs of victory and deliverance; when Babylon was asking for them to sing a song of Zion, GOD was speaking through the mouth of the captors to let the captives know that he's going to deliver them and give them victory.

Pay attention to your enemy, because GOD has the power to speak through their mouth to give you a word that he's about to deliver you. GOD will make people who don't like you prophecy to you.

In everything that this pastor thought he had taken from me, he wasn't able to take my ability to praise and worship. He told one of the ministers that he was going to destroy Hayes. I contacted the bishop who sent this man down. I contacted the organization that I had paid all this money to, all the so-called dues, and when this man did what he did, the organization did nothing. I was hurt and I was surprised. I spoke to the deacons of the church, the ministers, and I let them know that I was innocent. They did nothing.

One particular Bible study night, I decided to stay

home. The pastor called my wife into his office and began to tell her that she was Abigail and I was Nabal. When she came home she told me what he said, and I asked my wife, "Do you fully understand what he said to you?"

Abigail interceded for her husband Nabal; David was coming to kill him because he had offended David. I became angry all over again, because now the pastor was sending subliminal threats through my wife. The time was approaching for me to be ordained, and because some officials around me did not want the pastor to hold up my ordination another year, I was told that I needed to take a lie detector test to prevent him from holding me back.

My father took me to take the test, which was one of the most humiliating times of my life. Here I was with wires strapped across my chest and my stomach, all because a pastor lied on me and sought to destroy what GOD had planned for my life. A heavyset Caucasian man began asking me questions: he asked me if my name was Deon Hayes, he asked me my address, he asked me some more questions, and then he asked me if I canceled choir rehearsal. I said yes, and then he asked me, "Did you tell your pastor that you canceled the choir rehearsal?" I said yes. They began to take wires off me and I heard him tell my father, "This young man passed without a doubt; there is no way he lied. It's a shame he would even have to go through this."

I broke down crying. I couldn't believe that I was taking a lie detector test, not for murder, but because a pastor lied on me about a choir rehearsal and he had the power to hold me back from receiving my credentials. With tears flowing down my face I told my dad, "If this is what I have to go through for ministry, I don't want it."

Word got back to the pastor that I had passed the lie detector test, and the next Sunday he started his sermon off by talking about how easy it is to beat a lie detector test. I couldn't believe it. I was outdone, but I wasn't leaving. I refused to run. I sat in the front row, not to be disrespectful but to take a stand, to let the people know that I was innocent and I did nothing wrong. As the pastor was preaching he couldn't look my way. I was sitting in the right side of the church, and every Sunday he preached to the left side of the church. I guess he couldn't take it anymore.

One day my wife and I were sitting in the car in the parking lot of our town home, discussing the situation, and I was telling her that I couldn't believe this was happening to me. It was very stressful. I barely had enough energy left from fighting the injustice that I had received in the courtroom, and now the place that I normally would turn to for strength was against me, and those who believed me were silent in the matter. I looked up and saw a man coming from the front door of our home to the car. I noticed a badge on his belt. He asked, "Are you Deon Hayes?" I said yes, and he said, "You've been served. If you come on the church grounds again you will be arrested."

Here I was, in the middle of fighting for my lawsuit, and the church that I gave my all to had just put me out, not for being disrespectful, not for fighting, not for stealing money, but because the pastor could no longer preach with me in the front row.

My father called our district elder who was over our church, and he called the pastor, but the pastor refused to accept his calls, nor would he return his calls. One Tuesday evening, the district elder called and told me not to return to that church. I said, "What about my ordination? How am I going to receive my credentials? What about all the money I spent to become licensed and ordained?" This was challenging because the guidelines stated that your pastor had to sign off for you to be ordained, and my pastor had held my ordination up for two years. He was able to get away with this and not be held accountable. The district elder said, "Son, don't worry about it. Come to my church in Bradley, Illinois, and I'll place you under my care. I will act as your pastor to make sure you get ordained. GOD has a plan for you."

CHAPTER 10

Keep Your Hands Clean and Behave Yourself Wisely

I couldn't believe that this pastor was able to do what he did and there was no accountability. The organization that we belonged to did nothing. I paid my dues and fees required to belong to the organization and to be ordained by the organization, and they did nothing to protect me. I felt as if they protected him, knowing what he did was wrong. That day I lost respect for the organization and I would never be a part of something like that again.

One day GOD spoke to me and told me to make sure what happened to me didn't happen to anyone else. At the time I didn't know that GOD was going to give me a great church to pastor. I just remembered those words that GOD said to me, and I knew it meant that he wanted me to protect people, protect their purpose, help them get to their destiny.

I kept having these recurring dreams about being in a

jungle. I had one foot on a branch and I was holding it down as the people were passing over. I would wake up and tell my wife, "I think GOD wants me to be an actor." It looked like something from a movie. Now that I see where I am today, GOD wasn't calling me into acting; he was showing me that I would be leading the people out of the wilderness into a prepared place.

I had read about David and Saul. I never knew that I would see the story play out in my own life. I started to study the story of David and Saul, and I saw many comparisons between myself and this pastor. One particular scripture that stood out was Psalms 18:20. "The Lord rewarded me according to my righteousness: according to the cleanness of my hands hath he recompensed me."

The word "recompense" means an award for damages suffered.

I kept that scripture close to my heart. I knew GOD was going to bless me for what I went through, because what I went through wasn't my fault. GOD had a plan. I don't know why he chose me, but I'm so glad that he did. Notice that particular scripture says that GOD recompensed him according to the cleanness of his hands. The reward came because David kept his hands clean.

First Samuel 18:14-15 says, "And David behaved himself wisely in all his ways; and the Lord was pleased with him, when Saul saw that David behaved himself very wisely, he was afraid of him."

This explains why the pastor had to put me out of the ministry. My conduct scared him; he knew he lied on me, he knew he tried to stop the purpose that GOD had on my life, and he was expecting me to respond in a way that would bring a reproach upon my character, but GOD was with me, instructing me every step of the way. And because GOD was with me, I behaved myself wisely. I don't hold any hate or animosity in my heart for the pastor or any of the people who refused to help me. I pray for him, and I thank him, because if he hadn't done what he did, I wouldn't be where I am today. If I had time I would preach to you a sermon entitled "A Lie Got Me Here." Understand what you're going through is for a purpose and a reason; you may not understand it now but in the future you will, and you will give GOD the glory if you hold on to GOD and be faithful to him.

When we don't move on GOD's command, sometimes he will use an enemy to make us move. The truth is, I was supposed to be gone from that church a long time ago, but I'm a loyalist—that's a good thing and a bad thing, because being a loyalist will make you hold on, but it will also make you hold on too long.

You may be going through a trying time where Satan is attacking you. He may even use saints of GOD, people with titles, and it may seem like they're getting away with it and there's no accountability. But the eyes of the Lord are everywhere, beholding the good and the evil. Whatever you do, make sure you behave yourself wisely and keep your hands clean.

CHAPTER 11

The Battle Was for You, but the Victory Was for the People

I was ordained in the July council of 2006. The bishop who said GOD placed me in his dream stood in front of me. I felt that he was remorseful for what happened to me; he never said anything and I never said anything, but deep down inside I knew he felt bad. By this time, the church had dismantled, and a lot of people had left and weren't going to church at all. As bad as I felt about what happened to me, I felt worse about the people who were scattered as a result of this pastor's actions. I would run into former members and them what church they were going to, and some would respond, "Nowhere, I'm waiting for you to start your church."

I knew that GOD had called me to pastor, but after everything I had gone through, I had lost my passion and desire for ministry. I still loved GOD but that desire was no longer there. I started my own business named Heavenscent, a cleaning company. I came up with brilliant strategies to promote my company and to secure contracts, but no matter what I did, I couldn't get a contract, I traveled, offered to do jobs at a discounted rate, but no one would give me a chance.

One day I decided to take a ride on my bike. Because of my injury, I couldn't play basketball and so bike riding became therapeutic for me. When I needed to think or get away I would ride my bike. I'll never forget this day. I was riding and I heard GOD say, "It's time." Through the hurt and through the pain, I told GOD, "Whatever you want me to do, I'll do it."

Shortly after this brief conversation with GOD, a pet company contacted me and told me that they would like to hire my company to clean a store that they had just purchased; they were preparing for opening day and needed it to be cleaned immediately. I agreed, and as I was preparing the figures in my mind to give them a quote, the pet store called and said they wanted to pay me five thousand dollars. I couldn't believe it. I couldn't secure a deal before, and the one and only contract that I was able to get was an offer for five thousand dollars. I didn't ask for this amount; this is what they wanted to give me. My wife turned to me and said, "Maybe GOD wants you to start your church."

I was numb, still in disbelief. I knew this opportunity was connected to GOD, because it came after I told GOD yes. You would be surprised how many doors GOD will open for you if you just tell him yes; even if you don't understand, learn to tell GOD yes and learn to trust the process. GOD's will is perfect. Have confidence in the fact that the

Holy Ghost has the ability to step into the future and see things you don't see while you're still in your present. When GOD chooses to bless you, even your doubt can't stop it.

My wife and I cleaned the entire building. It took a weekend to complete but we worked hard and we got it done, scrubbing walls, mopping floors. We were determined to get the job done and make the money to start our church.

When I received the check I went and purchased microphones and speakers. We didn't even have a building yet, but I trusted GOD. We rented a small conference room for seventy-five dollars, and on August 20, 2006, One Vision Worship Center was birthed. At the first service there were over 100 people. Going into this tenth year of ministry, I can truly say that thousands of lives have been impacted because of the grace of GOD. I've preached all over the world, and GOD has given me an anointing to free souls from the hand of the enemy, but what if I never said yes?

"Don't allow past pain to prevent you from the possibility of future love." GOD spoke this to me. I often think of the damage I would have caused to myself and others if I allowed what happened to stagnate me. But I'm here now, doing the will of GOD, and now I see why the pastor did what he did to me. He thought it was for his own selfish reason. Satan thought it was to stop the plan of GOD for my life, but GOD knew that it was only to propel me to my place of destiny. When I look back at all the people I have helped, the people who constantly tell me that their life has changed because of One Vision Worship Center, sometimes I get emotional. I realize that I didn't go through what I went through for nothing; it was for the people. Every attack, every lie, every truth, every hater, every frenemy, it was all to get me to this place, and I thank GOD for it all. It didn't make me bitter; it made me better, more compassionate, more understanding, and more patient.

When I go in my church, I just look around and I hear a voice say, "Look what GOD has done for you." I've been blessed so well that sometimes I forget what I been through, so I have to remind myself to stop and give GOD the glory. Not every pastor is not experiencing this, so to GOD be the glory; he chose me for this.

On New Year's Eve 2015, GOD told me, "I'm restarting your church." I thought that he meant he was going to remove people from positions. I had no idea he was going to remove people from the church. When the year came in, I didn't have to put any troublemakers out. GOD began to remove them. This was the most that I had seen people leave my church. Don't get me wrong, not everybody who left were troublemakers—my church membership never got low; GOD always kept it full—but for a minute I did wonder what was going on, and I heard GOD say, "Just trust me." I focused on GOD and engaged in my assignment, and before I knew it, I had a church full of people with sincere motives who truly love me and support the vision that GOD has given me. This is the best time of ministry that I have ever experienced, but it only came after GOD removed the wrong people out of my life. I'm not bitter, I'm better.

CHAPTER 12

I've Got Enough Faith to Change the Verdict

I was adjusting to my new life as pastor when I received a letter from the appellate court. It came in a blue envelope, and I felt knots in my stomach. I couldn't take another disappointment concerning this case. I was hesitant to open it, but the Spirit of GOD urged me to.

The letter said, "Mr. Hayes, we are writing this letter to let you know that you have won your appeal, and your case will be reinstated." I was so excited, I danced around the room. I couldn't wait to tell my wife, because I wanted her to know that GOD was with me and I didn't hear him wrong. I had won the appeal, but the case wasn't over yet. I had to do more research. I had to prepare for court. I had to motion the case back into court, and the court gave us a new trial date.

I was relieved to find out that a new judge was going to rule over the case this time. We went back and forth to court like the last time, and I was hoping that I didn't have any setbacks like last time, but something inside me was telling me that GOD was not going to let it end like that. When your faith is on trial, you have to constantly speak the words in the atmosphere that GOD is not going to let it end like this. Your words and your atmosphere are very important.

In the 37th chapter of Ezekiel, GOD took Ezekiel to a valley of dry bones, and he asked him, "Can these bones live?" Ezekiel responded, "GOD, you know."

GOD told him to prophesy upon the bones; he prophesied, he heard a noise, there was a shaking, and the bones came together. The sinews and the flesh came up on the bones, and the skin covered them. But the Bible says there was no breath in them. Next GOD told him to prophesy to the wind, the atmosphere, and command them to breathe upon the bones that they may live. He did as he was commanded and breath came into the bones and they stood up upon their feet, an exceeding great army.

But life didn't come back in them until he prophesied to the wind.

The wind is made up of oxygen, nitrogen, carbon dioxide, methane, and helium; in other words, when you speak into the atmosphere, you're speaking to the elements that give and sustain life. Don't hold your words in, but open your mouth and make a declaration that flows from your heart.

Every court date that I had, I dressed in a sharp, conservative suit, like I had money already. A notice came in the mail informing me of my next court date, and when I arrived at the appointed courtroom, this time it was only the judge, the fitness center attorney, and me.

I had some major concerns because I didn't have any witness statements, I didn't have the doctor reports, and I didn't have any paperwork from the case because I had given everything to the paralegal who had mysteriously disappeared.

I began to argue the case, and I was nervous, hoping that the judge didn't ask for any records or paperwork, because I had nothing. I was standing there praying, "GOD, please don't let the judge ask me for proof." I had nothing, but I began to attack and not let up, arguing my case for willful and wanton conduct, pattern of behavior, and claims of witness statements. GOD was speaking in my ear. My heart was racing, sweat dripping down the side of my forehead, my shirt drenched from the intensity of the fight. Just when I was about to put the final hammer down, the defense attorney told the judge they would like to settle the case. I wanted to scream "Thank you, JESUS" at the top of my lungs. We went into the room to discuss settlement, and to my surprise the attorney had the check with him already, inside of his suit pocket; that's how life is. You're pleading your case, almost panicking, and GOD has the check already written out.

We came out and we talked to the judge, explaining that we had settled the case. The judge issued me a warning not to disclose the settlement amount. All I can say is GOD did it. The defense lawyer turned to the judge and said, "Your

Honor, for the record I would like to say Mr. Hayes was the hardest opponent that I have ever had in my life."

I was honored, but I wasn't his opponent. I was just an ambassador, a voice for GOD here on this earth, to teach the world what happens when you believe GOD for things that don't make sense.

www.ingramcontent.com/pod-product-compliance
Lightning Source LLC
La Vergne TN
LVHW021544080426
835509LV00019B/2833